INSIDE THE NBA

UTAH JAZZ

BY JONATHAN AVISE

SportsZone

An Imprint of Abdo Publishing
abdobooks.com

abdobooks.com

Published by Abdo Publishing, a division of ABDO, PO Box 398166, Minneapolis, Minnesota 55439.

Printed in China.
052022
092022

THIS BOOK CONTAINS RECYCLED MATERIALS

Cover Photo: Rick Bowmer/AP Images
Interior Photos: Melinda Nagy/Shutterstock Images, 1; Gene Sweeney Jr./Getty Images Sport/Getty Images, 4, 6, 9; Rick Bowmer/AP Images, 11; Focus on Sport/Getty Images Sport/Getty Images, 12, 15, 25, 34; Rich Pedroncelli/AP Images, 16; Vince Bucci/AFP/Getty Images, 19; Ezra Shaw/Getty Images Sport/Getty Images, 20; Todd Kirkland/Getty Images Sport/Getty Images, 21; Focus on Sport/Getty Images, 22; Mitchell Layton/Getty Images Sport/Getty Images, 26; Mark Terrill/AP Images, 28; George Frey/AFP/Getty Images, 29; Alex Goodlett/Getty Images Sport/Getty Images, 31; Roberto Borea/AP Images, 37; Paul Buck/AFP/Getty Images, 38; Kevork Djansezian/Getty Images Sport/Getty Images, 41

Editor: Charlie Beattie
Series Designer: Joshua Olson

Library of Congress Control Number: 2021951657

Publisher's Cataloging-in-Publication Data

Names: Avise, Jonathan, author.
Title: Utah Jazz / by Jonathan Avise
Description: Minneapolis, Minnesota : Abdo Publishing, 2023 | Series: Inside the NBA | Includes online resources and index.
Identifiers: ISBN 9781532198465 (lib. bdg.) | ISBN 9781098272111 (ebook)
Subjects: LCSH: Utah Jazz (Basketball team)--Juvenile literature. | Basketball--Juvenile literature. | Professional sports--Juvenile literature. | Sports franchises--Juvenile literature.
Classification: DDC 796.32364--dc23

TABLE OF
CONTENTS

CHAPTER ONE

A NEW JAZZ GENERATION

In the pressure-packed National Basketball Association (NBA) playoffs, a team needs its best players to rise to the occasion. The Utah Jazz got just that in their 2018 playoff series against the Oklahoma City Thunder. Unfortunately for the Jazz, the Thunder's star player stepped up too.

The teams met in the first round. After Utah jumped out to a 3–1 series lead, Oklahoma City clawed one back in Game 5. The Thunder needed another win in Game 6. Otherwise they were going home.

Oklahoma City was carrying the momentum. It had come back from a big deficit to win Game 5. The Thunder also had some of the NBA's best players in Russell Westbrook and Paul George. Utah was no slouch, though. In rookie guard Donovan Mitchell, the Jazz had a rising star of their own.

Utah Jazz guard Donovan Mitchell reacts after hitting a three-pointer against the Oklahoma City Thunder in Game 6 of the 2018 Western Conference playoffs.

Mitchell, *center*, and Thunder guard Russell Westbrook, *left*, thrilled fans as they dueled throughout the series.

Vivint Arena, Utah's home floor, was filled to the brim and roaring. But it was Mitchell who left his Thunder opponents' ears ringing. His play rose above the rest of the noise.

At 21, Mitchell was in his first NBA season after two years at the University of Louisville. He was picked by the Denver Nuggets thirteenth overall in the 2017 NBA Draft. But that night, the Jazz swung a trade for the young guard.

It was a great move for Utah. Mitchell had a strong debut. He averaged more than 20 points per game and was named to the league's All-Rookie team.

Westbrook, on the other hand, was 29. The Thunder point guard had won NBA scoring titles, had been named Most Valuable Player (MVP), and had guided the Thunder to an NBA Finals. As Game 6 continued, though, Mitchell went toe-to-toe with the established star.

TOUGH START

It was a slow start for both the rookie guard and the Jazz. Mitchell made just a single shot in the first quarter. After 12 minutes, the Thunder held a 22–18 lead. Utah battled back in the second quarter to tie the game at halftime. But the Jazz were struggling to stop Westbrook. He shot over defenders from outside. He streaked past them on his way to the hoop. At halftime he had a game-high 15 points.

Mitchell was Utah's only answer to Westbrook's stellar play. And Jazz coach Quin Snyder knew it. In a first-half huddle, he told Mitchell it was time to step up. "We're going to win this game, and you're going to go off," Snyder told his young star.

"Sometimes the team needs a guy to take things on his shoulders," Snyder told the media after the game.

SECOND-HALF SHOWDOWN

It took until the third quarter, but Mitchell put Snyder's words into action. Just 10 seconds into the second half, Mitchell's layup put Utah up 43–41. It kicked off a spectacular quarter of scoring for both Mitchell and Westbrook.

Mitchell drained a 25-foot three-pointer two possessions later. The next time down the floor, he dropped in a layup. Westbrook responded with a three-pointer of his own. But Mitchell answered right back. After the flurry, it was 51–46 Utah. Mitchell had racked up 10 second-half points in less than three minutes of action.

Behind the rookie, Utah was building a lead. When Mitchell hit another deep three-pointer with 6:33 left in the quarter, the Jazz were up 62–52. He was answering everything Westbrook threw at Utah's defense. When Westbrook cut the lead to eight points with 3:27 left in the third, Mitchell called for the ball at the other end. Driving straight at George on the left block, Mitchell charged to the rim. As George tried to slap down on the ball, Mitchell scooped a layup from his waist. It banked in as he went flying out of bounds. George was called for a foul.

Mitchell had made eight consecutive shots to start the third quarter. Then he stepped up to the free-throw line and knocked down his foul shot. It was 72–61 Utah.

Mitchell averaged 24.4 points per game during the playoffs in 2017–18, up from 20.5 points per game in the regular season.

"I was in a different mode," Mitchell said after the game. "It was crazy."

Mitchell missed his final two shots of the quarter, but his numbers were still amazing. He was 8-for-10 from the field for 22 points. The rookie had hit all three of his three-point shots. When he wasn't hitting from outside, he knocked down a combination of tough layups in traffic and difficult floaters as he spun and twisted to the rim.

Record Breaker

Donovan Mitchell made four playoff trips in his first four seasons. And the dynamic guard was also setting Jazz playoff scoring records. During a 2020 playoff game against the Denver Nuggets, Mitchell racked up 57 points in an overtime loss. It was the third-most points ever scored in an NBA playoff game. And it broke the Jazz's single-game playoff scoring record of 50 set by Karl Malone in 2000.

COOL IN THE CLUTCH

It nearly wasn't enough. Westbrook answered with 20 points of his own. The teams were still close late in the fourth quarter. Utah led 94–91 with six seconds left when Mitchell was fouled. Shaking off the pressure, he knocked down both shots. The rookie was 5-for-5 from the line.

When the game was over, Westbrook had 46 points. That was eight more than Mitchell's 38. But Utah's star rookie had something even more important. The Jazz had held on for a 96–91 victory. They had won the game and were moving on.

Mitchell celebrates with Jazz fans at Vivint Arena after Utah defeated the Thunder in Game 6.

Mitchell's performance marked his third 30-point game in the series. That made him just the third rookie in the previous 35 years of the NBA to do that in a playoff round. The other two were Hall-of-Famers Michael Jordan and Alonzo Mourning.

Utah's run ended in the next round with a loss to the favored Houston Rockets. But Mitchell had announced that the Jazz were back on the big stage.

CHAPTER TWO

SWEET MUSIC IN UTAH

Utah is a place known for its scenic landscapes. Snow-capped mountains soar in the state's north. And in the south, lonely deserts stretch toward the horizon. But the state is not known for jazz music. So, how did Utah's NBA team end up with a name like that?

The team didn't always play in the shadow of Utah's Wasatch Mountains. The Jazz's history began far south of the Great Salt Lake. The team first tipped off on the banks of the mighty Mississippi River in Louisiana.

The NBA added New Orleans as an expansion team in 1974, bringing the league to 18 teams. A fan contest helped land on the new team's name: Jazz, for the city's world-famous style of music.

However, unlike the city's talented musicians, the new team didn't play well. For five seasons in New Orleans the Jazz

Jazz forward Adrian Dantley looks to drive against the Washington Bullets in 1980.

Before the Music

Utah had a professional basketball team before the Jazz arrived in 1979. It just wasn't in the NBA. The Utah Stars played in the American Basketball Association (ABA) from 1970 to 1975. The Stars won the 1971 ABA championship by beating the Kentucky Colonels 4–3 in a best-of-seven series.

struggled to find their rhythm on the court. They finished last or second-to-last in their division each season. The Jazz never qualified for the playoffs during that time.

Another problem the team faced was the arena it called home in New Orleans. The Louisiana Superdome was a massive football stadium for the New Orleans Saints. It seated 19,000 for basketball games. The Jazz struggled to get half that amount to show up. It made the huge stadium feel like a cavern.

Jazz owners also strained to make enough money in New Orleans. In 1979 team owner Sam Battistone began looking to other cities. And soon the Jazz were headed west. Where they landed was a surprise to some.

THE GREAT SALT LAKE

Battistone received approval for the move to Salt Lake City in June 1979. That left little time before the start of the 1979–80 NBA season. So the team's New Orleans name stuck—the Utah Jazz.

"We didn't have time to change the name," Battistone later said.

More struggles awaited the Jazz in Utah, however. The team remained near the bottom of the standings during its early years in Salt Lake City. Once again, the Jazz were rumored to be on the move. Sunny Miami and snowy Minneapolis were talked about as the team's next home. Because of that, the team often struggled to draw fans.

However, a change was just around the corner. A franchise-best 45-win season in 1983–84 earned Utah a Midwest Division championship. Suddenly the Jazz were on the rise. Utah reached the playoffs for the first time. It was the start of an impressive 20-year postseason streak.

Guard Darrell Griffith (35) played his entire 10-season NBA career in Utah.

High-scoring Adrian Dantley was a big reason for the Jazz's improvement. He joined the team in a 1979 trade. The 6-foot-5-inch forward averaged more than 30 points per game from

John Stockton (12) and Karl Malone played 1,412 games together, more than any other pair of teammates in NBA history.

1981–82 through 1983–84. And 1981 NBA Rookie of the Year Darrell Griffith was busy slamming home dunks in support.

STOCKTON TO MALONE

Despite more success on the court, the Jazz were struggling off it. Battistone was losing money. Salt Lake City was the smallest city in the NBA. It was struggling to support the team.

A local auto dealer named Larry Miller came to the rescue in 1985. He bought half the team. A year later, Battistone was on the verge of selling the Jazz to a group that once again wanted to move the team to Minneapolis. Instead, Miller bought Battistone's share. By 1986 he was the team's sole owner.

He had saved the Jazz for Salt Lake City. Of course, it helped that the team had just drafted two future Hall-of-Fame players.

Karl Malone and John Stockton formed one of the most famous partnerships in NBA history. Malone was a powerful forward out of Louisiana Tech University. Stockton was a quick point guard from Gonzaga University.

The dynamic duo never missed the playoffs during their Jazz careers together. Stockton was the team's conductor on the floor. His passing helped set up other Jazz teammates to score. And Malone became one of the best scorers and rebounders in the league.

The "Stockton to Malone" connection helped muscle Utah up the NBA's Western Conference standings. The rest of the NBA was forced to take note of Utah. But each spring, the team kept coming up short. Trips to the Western Conference finals in 1992, 1994, and 1996 marked exciting postseason runs, but the Jazz could never advance to the NBA Finals.

The Jazz finally broke through in 1997. Stockton hit

More for Malone

Karl Malone wasn't only the Jazz's greatest-ever scorer. He was one of the most productive point-getters in NBA history. Malone's 36,928 points ranked second all-time when he retired after the 2003–04 season. Only Lakers great Kareem Abdul-Jabbar had scored more points.

a buzzer-beater in Game 6 of the Western Conference finals against the Houston Rockets. This sent the Jazz to the NBA Finals for the very first time.

OH-SO-CLOSE

Utah's opponents for the 1997 NBA championship were the fearsome Chicago Bulls. The Bulls had won the 1996 title after an NBA record 72-win season. Coming into the 1997 Finals against the Jazz, Chicago had won a league-best 69 games in the regular season. The Bulls featured Michael Jordan, whom many considered the best player in league history.

The Jazz lost the first two games of the series in Chicago but rebounded to win the next two at home. However, the visiting Bulls won Game 5 in Salt Lake City and finished the series with a Game 6 win at home.

Afterward, both Utah and Chicago stormed through the 1997–98 season. Both teams won 62 regular-season games as well as their conference titles. They met for a second time in the 1998 NBA Finals.

Once again the series went six games. But this time, the Jazz were a victim of another famous shot. Utah led 86–85 as the clock ticked down in Game 6. If the Jazz could have held on, they would have forced a winner-take-all Game 7.

Unfortunately, the ball was in Jordan's hands. With five seconds left, he rose up and hit a 17-foot jump shot. It clinched

Karl Malone goes up for a finger-roll over three Chicago Bulls defenders during the 1997 NBA Finals.

the 87–86 lead and the Bulls' third-straight NBA championship. It was a second-straight heartbreaking Finals loss for Jazz fans.

Stockton, Malone, and their Jazz teammates never came that close to a title again. Utah extended its string of playoff appearances for five more seasons. But the Jazz did not advance further than the conference semifinals in any of those seasons.

Deron Williams attempts a jump shot during the 2010 playoffs against the Denver Nuggets.

Stockton's career came to an end after Utah was knocked out of the playoffs with a five-game loss to the Sacramento Kings in the opening round of the 2003 playoffs. Malone left Utah that offseason to play his final season with the Los Angeles Lakers. Neither ever won their hoped-for NBA title.

MODERN MUSIC

The pair's exit delivered a big blow to Utah. The Jazz missed the playoffs in 2004. Two more poor seasons followed. But the team still had its Hall-of-Fame coach, Jerry Sloan. A rebuilt roster of young players returned the Jazz to their winning ways in 2006–07.

Utah made it back to the postseason that year. The Jazz advanced all the way to the Western Conference finals. There they fell 4–0 to the eventual NBA champion San Antonio Spurs.

After three more playoff appearances, the Jazz ran into trouble in 2010–11. Sloan decided to retire with the team sitting

31–23 in February. Two weeks after Sloan resigned, star point guard Deron Williams was traded to the New Jersey Nets. The team ended up missing the playoffs. It failed to qualify in four of the next five years as well.

However, a new generation of stars soon began making Utah a championship contender again. Guard Donovan Mitchell debuted for the Jazz in the 2017–18 season. The energetic scorer immediately made an impact. And with Mitchell partnered with All-Star center Rudy Gobert, the Jazz again became a regular in the NBA's postseason.

Exciting players like Mitchell, Gobert, guard Jordan Clarkson, and forward Bojan Bogdanović took Utah back to the top. In the 2020–21 regular season, the team won the Northwest Division and finished first in the Western Conference. Jazz fans hoped they would soon be singing about another trip to the NBA Finals.

Shooting guard Jordan Clarkson became a reliable scorer for the Jazz after joining the team in 2019.

CHAPTER THREE

MUSIC MAKERS

Pete Maravich loved to put on a show. The New Orleans Jazz's first star was nicknamed "Pistol Pete" for his circus passes, behind-the-back dribbles, and big scoring numbers.

Maravich had starred at nearby Louisiana State University. When the NBA awarded an expansion team to New Orleans in 1974, the team's front office searched for a star to draw fans. They wanted Maravich as the big attraction. A trade brought him to the brand-new team, and Pistol Pete became the Jazz's very first player.

From 1974 to 1979, he put on a spectacular show for anyone watching. As a team, the newly formed Jazz struggled on the court. But Maravich shone as the face of the franchise. He was at the peak of his powers during those years. The 6-foot-5-inch guard led the league in scoring during the 1976–77 season by averaging 31.1 points per game. He scored 40 or more points

The freewheeling Pete Maravich brought plenty of highlights but few wins to the Jazz's early seasons in New Orleans.

Voice of the Jazz

For almost 40 seasons, Jazz fans who tuned in to games heard one voice. Rodney "Hot Rod" Hundley was the first TV and radio announcer for the brand-new New Orleans Jazz in 1974. He followed the team to Utah and went on to call 3,051 Jazz games until he retired in 2009.

in 13 of the 72 games he played that year.

Maravich battled injuries throughout his career, however. By the time the Jazz left New Orleans for Salt Lake City, all those bumps and bruises had taken their toll. Maravich followed the team to Utah and spent part of his last season in a Jazz jersey before retiring. His freewheeling style on the court had helped make professional basketball more open and exciting.

MOUNTAIN MEN

A new high-scoring Jazz star emerged as Maravich retired. Adrian Dantley became the Jazz's new team leader starting in 1979–80. He arrived in a trade from the Los Angeles Lakers to a Jazz team desperate to find success. Dantley, nicknamed "the Teacher," was a 6-foot-5-inch small forward.

Dantley topped the league in scoring twice while wearing a Jazz jersey. Between 1981–82 and 1983–84, Dantley averaged more than 30 points per game. He could find the net from anywhere on the court. His strength allowed him to back down much bigger players near the hoop. Farther from the rim, his sweet jump shot sent basketballs swishing through the net. Dantley also had a knack for drawing fouls. That earned him many trips to the free-throw line where he padded his point totals.

Disagreements with head coach Frank Layden led to Dantley's exit from the team before the 1986–87 season began. But in seven seasons with the Jazz, Dantley made the All-Star team six times.

Mark Eaton wasn't known for his offensive skills. But he was a giant center and a dominant defensive player. During his 11 years in a Jazz uniform, Eaton became one of the league's most feared defenders.

Mark Eaton averaged 5.6 blocks per game during the 1984–85 season.

Eaton stood a towering 7 feet, 4 inches and dominated the area near the basket. His titanic size helped the center swat away opponents' shots. He retired with 3,064 blocked shots, which was an NBA record at the time. He also set a record for

John Stockton led the NBA in assists every season from 1987–88 to 1995–96.

the most blocked shots in a season with 456 in 1984–85. That year he won the first of his two NBA Defensive Player of the Year Awards.

THE PICK-AND-ROLL PAIR

He was called the perfect point guard. John Stockton had speed, agility, and unequaled passing ability.

Other players were flashier on the court than Stockton. But few could command the game like the 6-foot-1 guard. Using a variety of bounce passes and layups, the 10-time All-Star was the Jazz's floor leader.

Gonzaga University in Spokane, Washington, became a college basketball power in the 2000s. But that wasn't the case when Stockton played there in the early 1980s. The guard was not well known when Utah selected him with the sixteenth pick of the 1984 NBA Draft. "Who is this guy?" many wondered, as NBA Commissioner David Stern announced the selection. Critics said Utah's newest player was too small. Jazz fans on hand at New York City's Madison Square Garden even booed. It didn't take long for Stockton to change their minds.

Stockton's unselfish style of play helped to make him the NBA's all-time leader in assists, with 15,806. It is a record unlikely ever to be broken. His passing ability helped unlock opposing defenses and lead the NBA in assists nine times.

Karl Malone averaged a career-high 31.0 points per game in 1989–90.

His skills weren't limited to offense. The gritty guard was a tenacious defender too. Stockton retired as the NBA's all-time leader in steals with 3,265.

In Stockton's 19 seasons wearing a Jazz uniform, the team never missed the playoffs. And the durable guard played in each of the team's 82 games in 16 of those seasons.

One year after the Jazz drafted Stockton, they took power forward Karl Malone thirteenth overall. He immediately made an impact. His 14.9 points and 8.9 rebounds per game were good enough for voters to rank him third in Rookie of the Year voting in 1985–86.

It was the beginning of a perfect partnership. For 18 seasons as a member of the Jazz, Malone delivered the buckets off Stockton's passes. The Hall-of-Famer was one of the greatest scorers in NBA history. He averaged more than 25 points and 10 rebounds per game for a string of successful Jazz teams.

Using his size and brute strength, Malone overpowered opponents in the paint. He was a physical scorer under the basket and a punishing rebounder. But the big power forward's skills didn't stop in the paint. He could also run the court and sink jump shots over defenders farther away from the basket.

He earned the nickname "the Mailman" for his consistency. Malone scored nearly 37,000 points in his career. He was an

The fiery Jerry Sloan coached the Jazz for parts of 23 different seasons.

NBA All-Star 14 times. Twice, Malone was named the NBA MVP, in 1997 and 1999.

Stockton and Malone had most of their success running one of basketball's simplest plays—the pick and roll. After Malone set screens for Stockton, the point guard could find the big man anywhere on the floor with his precise passing. Sometimes Malone would roll to the basket for layups. Other times he would step out for outside shots. If no one picked up Stockton, he had the ability to knock down jumpers too. With so many options off one play, the duo was nearly unstoppable.

THE MEN IN CHARGE

After 20 games of the 1981–82 NBA season, the Jazz were just 8–12. Layden, the team's general manager, thought it might be time for a coaching change. Layden fired Tom Nissalke and took over the head coach position himself. While he went 17–45 the rest of the way, he and the Jazz didn't struggle much longer. Within two years, they were in the playoffs.

Layden brought in both Stockton and Malone. He then started the process that made both players superstars. It also turned Utah into a serious contender.

Layden was burned out on coaching by 1988. Just 17 games into the 1988–89 season, he resigned. Assistant coach Jerry Sloan took over. Sloan was a star guard with the Chicago Bulls in the 1960s and 1970s. He proved to be an even better coach.

Rudy Gobert, *right*, won his first NBA Defensive Player of the Year Award in 2017–18.

The talented Sloan took what Layden had started and made it better. In his first full season as coach in 1989–90, the Jazz won a team-record 55 games.

Sloan was still on the bench when Utah made both of its NBA Finals appearances. He then coached the team well into the new century, long after Stockton and Malone had left. He became the first NBA coach to win 1,000 games with one team.

Sloan finally stepped down 54 games into the 2010–11 season. It had been almost 30 years since the Jazz were

Jazzy Nicknames

Karl "the Mailman" Malone isn't the only Utah Jazz player who has delivered with a great nickname. There was "Pistol Pete" Maravich. And there was the rim-rattling Darrell Griffith, nicknamed "Dr. Dunkenstein." Newer Jazz players have some catchy nicknames too. Paris, France, has the Eiffel Tower. Utah has "the Stifle Tower." That's 7-foot-1-inch French center Rudy Gobert, who is known for his stifling defense.

coached by someone other than himself or Layden. In the 28 full seasons with one of the two men on the bench, Utah made the playoffs 24 times.

TWENTY-FIRST-CENTURY STARS

After Stockton and Malone had moved on, the Jazz needed new heroes in the mid-2000s. Utah had missed the playoffs three straight seasons when a new combination led the Jazz back in 2006–07. Point guard Deron Williams broke out that season, his second in the NBA. In three of the next four seasons, he averaged more than 18 points and 10 assists per game.

Playing Karl Malone to Williams's John Stockton was power forward Carlos Boozer. The 6-foot-9-inch native of Juneau, Alaska, made the first of two All-Star trips in 2006–07.

Boozer and Williams helped Utah to the playoffs for three more seasons before both moved on to other teams. Playing in the shadow of the legends who came before them, the pair kept Utah competitive in the West.

The Jazz's next guard/post combo of Donovan Mitchell and Rudy Gobert had something in common—both players were drafted by the Denver Nuggets.

Gobert came first. He was picked by Denver with the twenty-seventh selection in 2013. That night he was traded to the Jazz.

Like Eaton before him, Gobert is more noticeable at the defensive end of the floor. The French center is one of the NBA's best shot blockers. While Gobert stands 7 feet, 1 inch tall, his long arms stretch to a wingspan of 7 feet, 9 inches. That allows him to swallow up potential shooters near the basket. In addition to multiple Defensive Player of the Year awards, Gobert is a rebounding machine. He averaged 13.5 while making his first All-Star team in 2019–20.

While Gobert provides the defense, guard Donovan Mitchell piles up the points. Acquired from the Nuggets in another draft-night trade in 2017, Mitchell has been a scorer since his first day in the NBA. He averaged 20.5 points as a rookie to help the Jazz get back to the playoffs. Like Gobert, he made his first All-Star team in 2019–20.

The two Jazz stars helped the team finish with the best record in the Western Conference in 2020–21. As they looked to the future, Utah fans felt hopeful their team would be set at both ends of the floor for years to come.

JAZZ
22

CHAPTER FOUR

HITTING THE HIGH NOTES

The Jazz's early years on the court were fun to watch. Pete Maravich was busy zinging passes through his legs, around his back, and to teammates he couldn't even see. However, the team couldn't turn that fun into wins. The Jazz were regulars in the division basement. In the team's first nine seasons, they finished last or next-to-last each time.

"It would be Pete with 35 [points] and the Jazz 80 to the other team's 110," former general manager and coach Frank Layden once said. "Eventually, you've got to win."

In 1983–84 Utah's fortunes began to change. On the court, the team's star, Adrian Dantley, had returned from missing most of the previous season. High-scoring guard Darrell Griffith helped carry the scoring load. And sixth-man John Drew averaged almost 18 points a game off the bench.

Small forward John Drew joined the Jazz before the 1982–83 season and helped the team win its first playoff series a year later.

One season after winning just 30 of 82 games, the Jazz were the NBA's surprise team. A 15-win improvement was good enough for first place in the Midwest Division. That meant the Jazz, in their tenth season, were finally good enough for the NBA Playoffs.

There they snuck by the Denver Nuggets in the first round. Dantley scored 39 points to keep the team alive in Game 4. Then he knocked down 30 more to win Game 5 in the best-of-five series.

Utah fell in the next round to the Phoenix Suns. But a tradition had begun. The Jazz made the playoffs in each of the next 19 seasons.

The Queen of Basketball

In 1977 the New Orleans Jazz made a historic selection during the NBA Draft. In the seventh round, the Jazz selected a star player from Delta State University in Cleveland, Mississippi. Her name was Lusia Harris. One of the first stars of the women's game, Harris was the first woman to officially be drafted by an NBA team. Despite that, Harris never joined the Jazz on the floor. When she died in January 2022, the "Queen of Basketball" was still the only female draft pick in NBA history.

STARS AMONG STARS

On February 21, 1993, the All-Star show came to Utah for the first time. Future Hall-of-Famers like Michael Jordan, Shaquille O'Neal, and Patrick Ewing took the court for the Eastern Conference.

John Stockton, *left*, and Karl Malone hold up the MVP trophy after sharing the award at the 1993 All-Star Game.

Among those suiting up for the Western Conference on the Jazz's home court were two hometown heroes—power forward Karl Malone and point guard John Stockton. The famous partners did more than just wave hello to the Utah faithful in the crowd of 19,000.

The Jazz pair shone doing what they did every day in Utah. The powerful Malone poured on the offense for the Western Conference. He contributed 28 points and 10 rebounds in his 34 minutes on the floor. The quick and tenacious Stockton dished out 15 assists to his All-Star teammates.

Their efforts helped the Western All-Stars outlast their Eastern Conference opponents 135–132 in an exciting

John Stockton leaps into the air after hitting the game-winning three-pointer at the buzzer in Game 6 of the 1997 Western Conference finals.

overtime battle. The two teammates who shared so much success on the basketball court would share one more thing. Stockton and Malone were named the game's co–MVPs.

THE SHOT

In 1997, after 13 straight playoff appearances, the Utah Jazz had yet to make the NBA Finals. The team came close three times, losing in the Western Conference finals in 1992, 1994, and 1996. That unlucky run came to a close on May 29 with the greatest shot in team history.

John Stockton had been part of a dozen Utah playoff teams that fell short. By the 1996–97 season, he and the Jazz had had enough. They stormed through the regular season and won a team-record 64 games. Utah earned the top seed for the Western Conference playoffs. Then the Jazz rolled through the first two rounds.

However, the conference finals were a back-and-forth affair. Utah had won the first two games at home against the Houston Rockets. But the Rockets bounced back with a pair of wins on their home floor in Houston. The Jazz took Game 5 in Utah. They needed one more win to make the NBA Finals.

Game 6 was a hard-fought contest. Utah trailed Houston by 10 points with just under three minutes to play. But the Jazz rallied to draw even. As the clock ticked away to the final seconds, the score remained tied at 100–100. Utah guard Bryon Russell stood at center court looking to make an inbounds pass as Houston's crowd roared.

With just 2.8 seconds remaining, Russell found Stockton. The veteran received the ball and dribbled once as he moved just outside the three-point line. There, he launched his shot over defender Charles Barkley's outstretched arms.

The ball soared through the air and found its mark. As it sank through the hoop, Stockton leaped into the air in celebration in front of the suddenly silent Houston crowd. The Jazz had won and were moving on to the NBA Finals at last.

DEFYING GRAVITY

Since his college days at Louisville, Donovan Mitchell has been nicknamed "Spida," or "Spider." Like the superhero Spiderman, the high-powered guard can practically jump out of the gym.

Mitchell was invited to the 2018 NBA Slam Dunk Contest at that year's All-Star Game. Fans who didn't know the first-year player before certainly knew him after.

The 6-foot-1-inch Mitchell was launching himself like a rocket off the court. With his second dunk of the contest, he leaped over movie star Kevin Hart and others to slam the ball home. It earned him a perfect 50-point score from judges.

His third dunk earned another perfect score. Mitchell bounced the basketball off the backboard and jumped to catch it. He then swung the ball behind him like a windmill before smashing it through the hoop.

Wearing the jersey of former dunk champion Vince Carter, Mitchell clinched his own dunk contest win with his final dunk. Afterward, he stood proudly at center court holding his trophy.

"This is one of my favorite events of All-Star Weekend growing up as a kid watching it," the high-flying rookie said on television. "To win it, it's crazy."

It was also a sign of things to come for a player who was becoming one of the NBA's best. His exciting dunks and all-around scoring ability were ready to carry the Jazz into their next great era.

Donovan Mitchell leaps over actor Kevin Hart (in green) and others for a slam at the 2018 NBA Slam Dunk Contest.

TIMELINE

1974

The New Orleans Jazz begin play as the NBA's eighteenth franchise. The Jazz finish 23–59 during their first season.

1979

After five losing seasons in New Orleans, the franchise relocates to Salt Lake City.

1984

The Jazz win the Midwest Division and qualify for the NBA playoffs for the first time. The team drafts point guard John Stockton, a future Hall of Famer, in June.

1985

Utah drafts future Hall-of-Fame power forward Karl Malone.

1986

Larry H. Miller buys complete control of the Jazz from the team's original owners and cements the team's future in Utah.

1988

Jerry Sloan takes over as head coach from Frank Layden. Sloan goes on to coach the team until February 2011.

1991

The Jazz move from the NBA's smallest home arena, the Salt Palace, into the brand-new 18,000-seat Delta Center.

1993

The Jazz host the NBA All-Star Game. Hometown stars Malone and Stockton share the MVP Award.

1997

Utah makes its first appearance in the NBA Finals but loses the series 4–2 to the Chicago Bulls.

1998

The Jazz again advance to the NBA Finals but once again lose 4–2 to Chicago.

2003

Stockton retires and Malone leaves the team to spend his final season with the Los Angeles Lakers.

2007

The Jazz advance to their sixth Western Conference finals but are swept by the San Antonio Spurs.

2011

Jerry Sloan resigns in February after 23 years and more than 1,800 games as Utah's head coach.

2017

The Jazz return to the playoffs after a four-season absence. After the season, Utah gets point guard Donovan Mitchell in a draft-day trade.

2018

Mitchell wins the NBA Slam Dunk Contest during NBA All-Star Weekend in Los Angeles and finishes second in NBA Rookie of the Year voting.

2021

Utah finishes the regular season with the best record in the Western Conference and advances to the second round of the NBA playoffs.

TEAM FACTS

FRANCHISE HISTORY

New Orleans Jazz (1974–79)
Utah Jazz (1979–)

KEY PLAYERS

Thurl Bailey (1983–91)
Carlos Boozer (2004–10)
Adrian Dantley (1979–86)
Mark Eaton (1982–93)
Rudy Gobert (2013–)
Darrell Griffith (1980–91)
Gordon Hayward (2010–17)
Jeff Hornacek (1993–2000)
Andrei Kirilenko (2001–11)
Karl Malone (1985–2003)
Pete Maravich (1974–80)
Donovan Mitchell (2017–)
John Stockton (1984–2003)
Deron Williams (2005–11)

KEY COACHES

Frank Layden (1981–88)
Jerry Sloan (1988–2011)

HOME ARENAS

Loyola Field House (1974–75)
Municipal Auditorium (1974–75)
Louisiana Superdome (1975–79)
Salt Palace (1979–91)
Vivint Arena (1991–)
Formerly known as:
Delta Center (1991–2006)
Energy Solutions Arena (2006–15)

TEAM TRIVIA

NOTES ON A NOTE

The Jazz's unique logo is known as the J-note. It is a J in the shape of a musical note and includes a basketball. The symbol was created before the team's first season in New Orleans.

NAME GAME

More than 6,500 suggestions were submitted when the owners of New Orleans' new NBA team held a naming contest in 1974. Jazz was selected from a list of eight semifinalists. The others were Dukes, Crescents, Pilots, Cajuns, Blues, Deltas, and Knights.

NO TOP PICKS

Through 2021, the Jazz have never had the first overall pick in the NBA Draft held each year. Their highest pick came in the 1980 draft. They selected Darrell Griffith second overall from the University of Louisville.

THE BEAR

Utah's mascot is known as Jazz Bear. The costumed bear in a Utah Jazz uniform was introduced in 1994. He first appeared by sliding down a rope from the arena's ceiling high above the basketball court.

GLOSSARY

assist

A pass that leads directly to a basket.

commissioner

The chief executive of a sports league.

conference

A subset of teams within a sports league.

contender

A person or team that has a good chance at winning a championship.

deficit

The amount by which a team is trailing in a game.

draft

A system that allows teams to acquire new players coming into a league.

durable

Tough; in sports, a player who rarely suffers an injury.

expansion team

A new team that is added to an existing league.

general manager

An executive who runs a team and is responsible for finding and signing players.

postseason

Another word for playoffs; the time after the end of the regular season when teams play to determine a champion.

rookie

A professional athlete in his or her first year of competition.

tenacious

Unwilling to give up.

MORE INFORMATION

BOOKS

Flynn, Brendan. *The NBA Encyclopedia for Kids*. Minneapolis, MN: Abdo Publishing, 2022.

Mahoney, Brian. *GOATs of Basketball*. Minneapolis, MN: Abdo Publishing, 2022.

Ybarra, Andres. *Great Basketball Debates*. Minneapolis, MN: Abdo Publishing, 2019.

ONLINE RESOURCES

Booklinks NONFICTION NETWORK
FREE! ONLINE NONFICTION RESOURCES

To learn more about the Utah Jazz, please visit **abdobooklinks.com** or scan this QR code. These links are routinely monitored and updated to provide the most current information available.

INDEX

ABOUT THE AUTHOR

Jonathan Avise is a freelance writer who lives in Minneapolis with his wife.